WHERE DOES OUTER SPACE BEGIN?

WEATHER BOOKS FOR KIDS

Children's Earth Sciences Books

Speedy Publishing LLC
40 E. Main St. #1156
Newark, DE 19711
www.speedypublishing.com

f you want to go into outer space, how far do you have to go? There can be different answers! Read on and learn where outer space starts.

Inner space galaxy.

INNER SPACE AND OUTER SPACE

I f we want to figure out where outer space begins, we first have to decide what is, and isn't, "outer space". It's a little harder than figuring out where the inside of your house stops and the outside world starts.

Your house probably has solid walls, doors, windows, a floor, and a roof. Those things enclose the "inside" of your house. Between us and outer space there is no solid wall and no clear border. Where outer space starts is sort of a tricky question to answer.

Messier 82. Composite of Chandra, HST and Spitzer images. X-ray data recorded by Chandra appears in blue; infrared light recorded by Spitzer appears in red; Hubble's observations of hydrogen emission appear in orange, and the bluest visible light appears in yellow-green.

WHAT IS "OUTER SPACE"?

Outer space is the great, vast space in which the Sun, all the planets and moons, meteors and other objects move. It is a hard vacuum, which means there is no air or any other gas in noticeable amounts.

Space is not completely empty. It has a thin mix, or "plasma", of helium and hydrogen. Along with that there are magnetic fields, electromagnetic radiation, dust, cosmic rays, and "dark matter" that we don't even understand yet.

Earth and galaxy (Collage images from www.nasa.gov).

HOW HIGH CAN WE GO AND BE "INSIDE"?

[H]ere we are on the Earth, our home. We can be pretty sure this environment—the ground, the water, the air, the plants, and the animals—is not "outer space". So that's a start.

If we went down in a mine or the deepest basement of a big building, we would be going further into the Earth, not toward outer space, so that's the wrong direction!

So we must need to go up, toward the sky and beyond the sky, to get to a place where we can say with confidence, "Outer space starts here." But how far do we have to go?

The Baby Professor book *A Giant Shield* talks in more detail about the layers of our atmosphere, but let's look at a couple of those layers quickly now.

Standardized Temperature Profile An average temperature profile through the lower layers of the atmosphere.

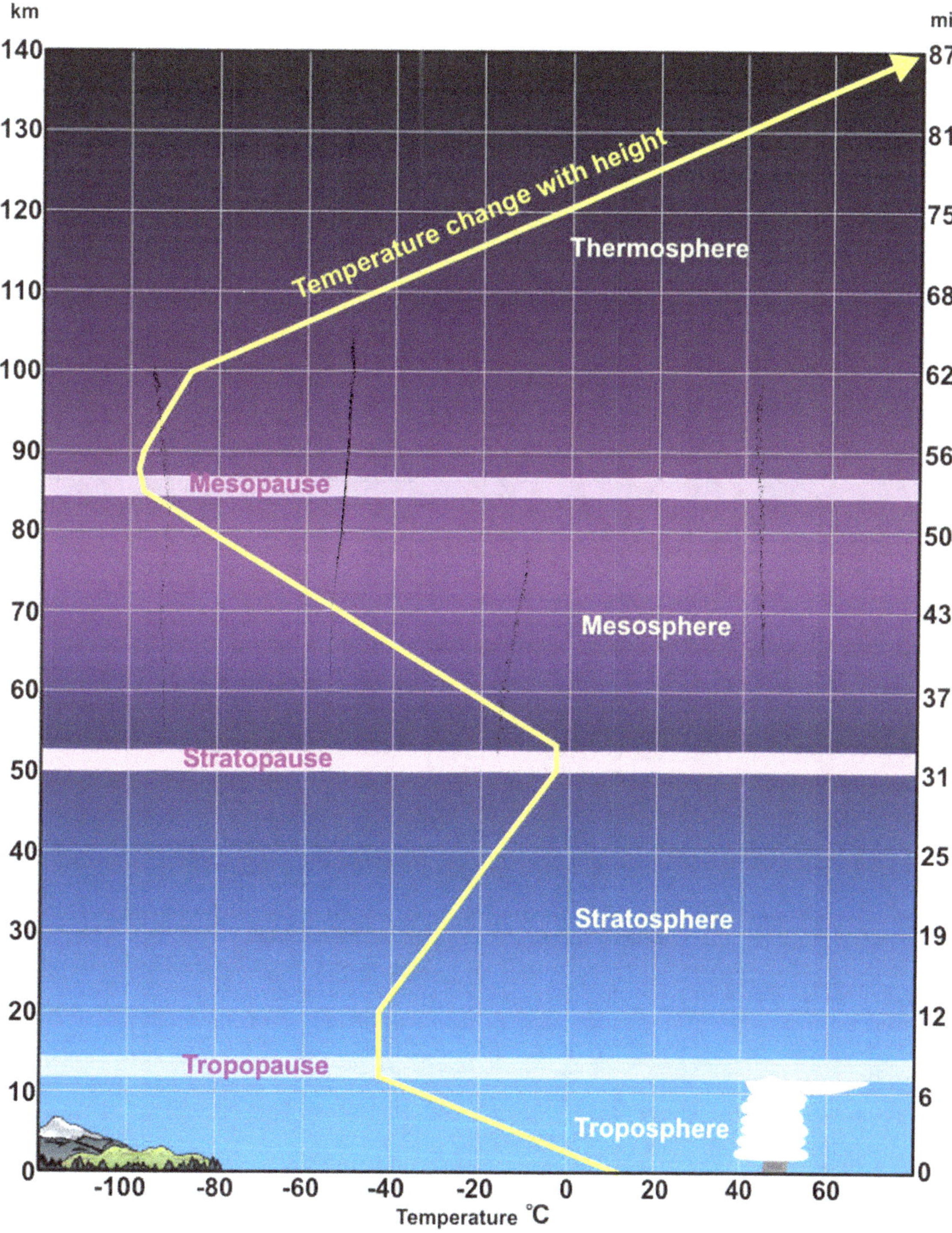

km
mi
140
130
120
110
100
90
80
70
60
50
40
30
20
10
0
87
81
75
68
62
56
50
43
37
31
25
19
12
6
0
Temperature change with height
Thermosphere
Mesopause
Mesosphere
Stratopause
Stratosphere
Tropopause
Troposphere
-100
-80
-60
-40
-20
0
20
40
60
Temperature °C

Troposphere

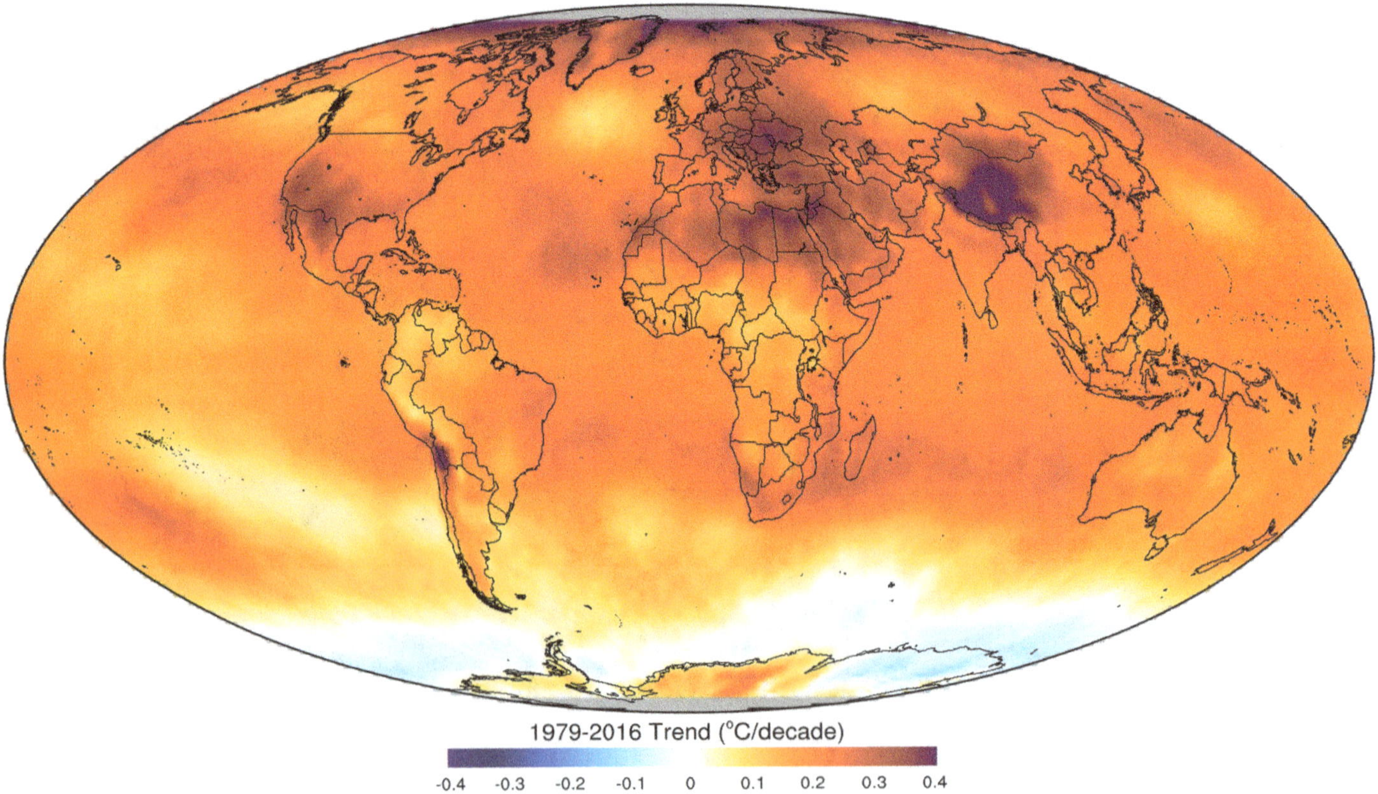

THE TROPOSPHERE

Almost all of us spend almost all of our lives in the very lowest layer, the troposphere. The troposphere is almost eleven miles thick. It has most of the oxygen in the atmosphere, most of the moisture, and almost all the weather. This is the environment we evolved in and that provides us with the air we need to breathe.

Even if we go only half-way to the top of the troposphere, walking up the highest mountain, Mount Everest (about six miles high), the air is so thin that most of us would find it hard to get enough oxygen. Mountain climbers going up Everest usually take a supply of oxygen tanks with them.

So, is the limit to "inner space" where the air gets too thin for us to breathe? Probably not, because there's a lot of clouds, wind, moisture, and weather events that happen higher than the top of Mount Everest and affect us down here at sea level.

So let's look further.

Stratosphere

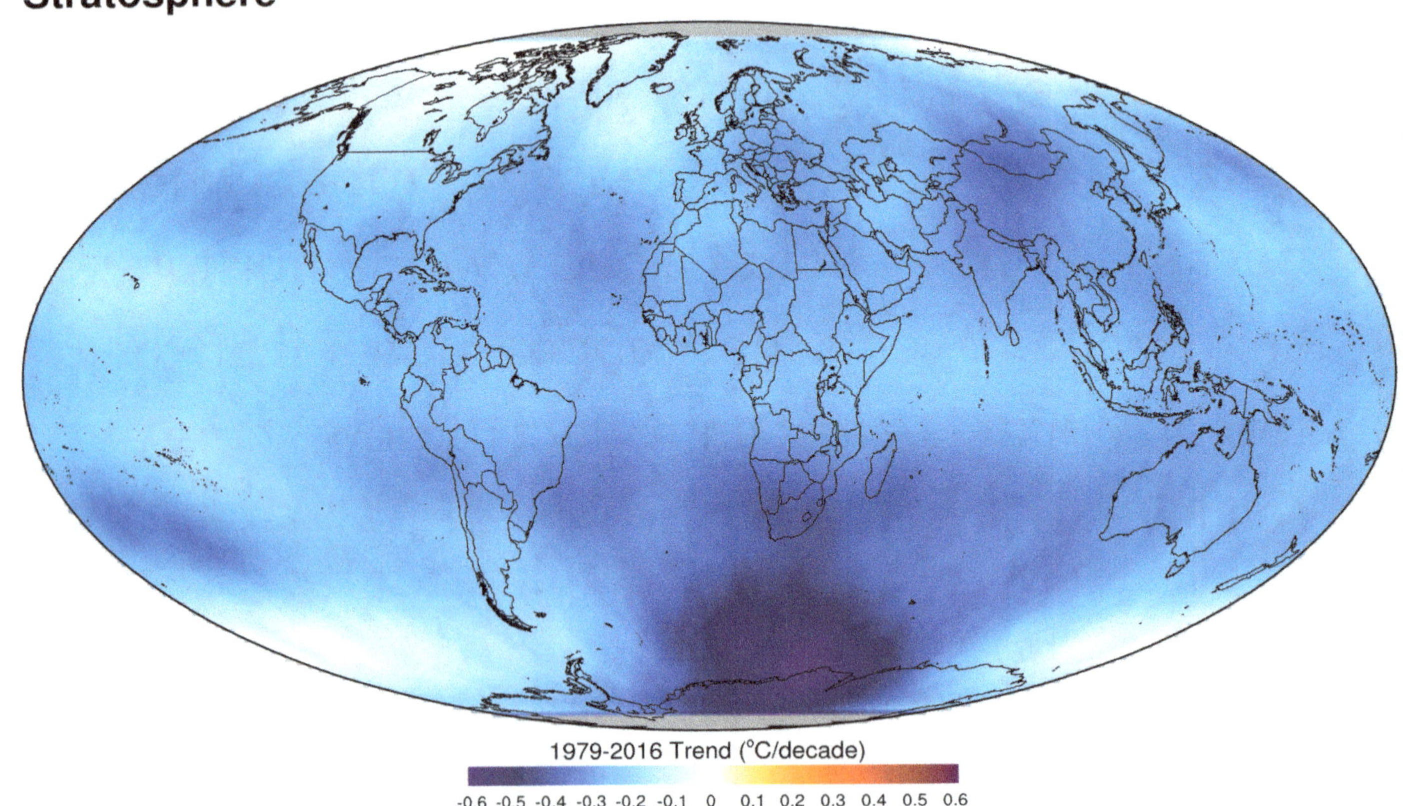

THE STRATOSPHERE

The next layer out from the Earth is the stratosphere. It reaches about thirty miles up from sea level. In this layer is the ozone layer that absorbs a lot of the Sun's energy. If we lived above the ozone layer without protection, we would not live long because our bodies could not survive what the Sun sends us.

Is that protective layer the line between our inner space, where we can live, and outer space where we would not survive? No, because we need yet another layer of protection.

THE MESOSPHERE

Space is not empty. It is full of debris, ranging from very small bits to chunks of rock the size of a small country. This stuff is all following different paths and orbits, and thousands of little pieces of dust, rock, and other material are on a collision course with our planet every day.

So why aren't rocks falling on our head all the time? They are moving so fast in relation to the Earth's movement that when they hit the next layer of the atmosphere, the mesosphere, almost all of them burn up.

Atmospheric layers.

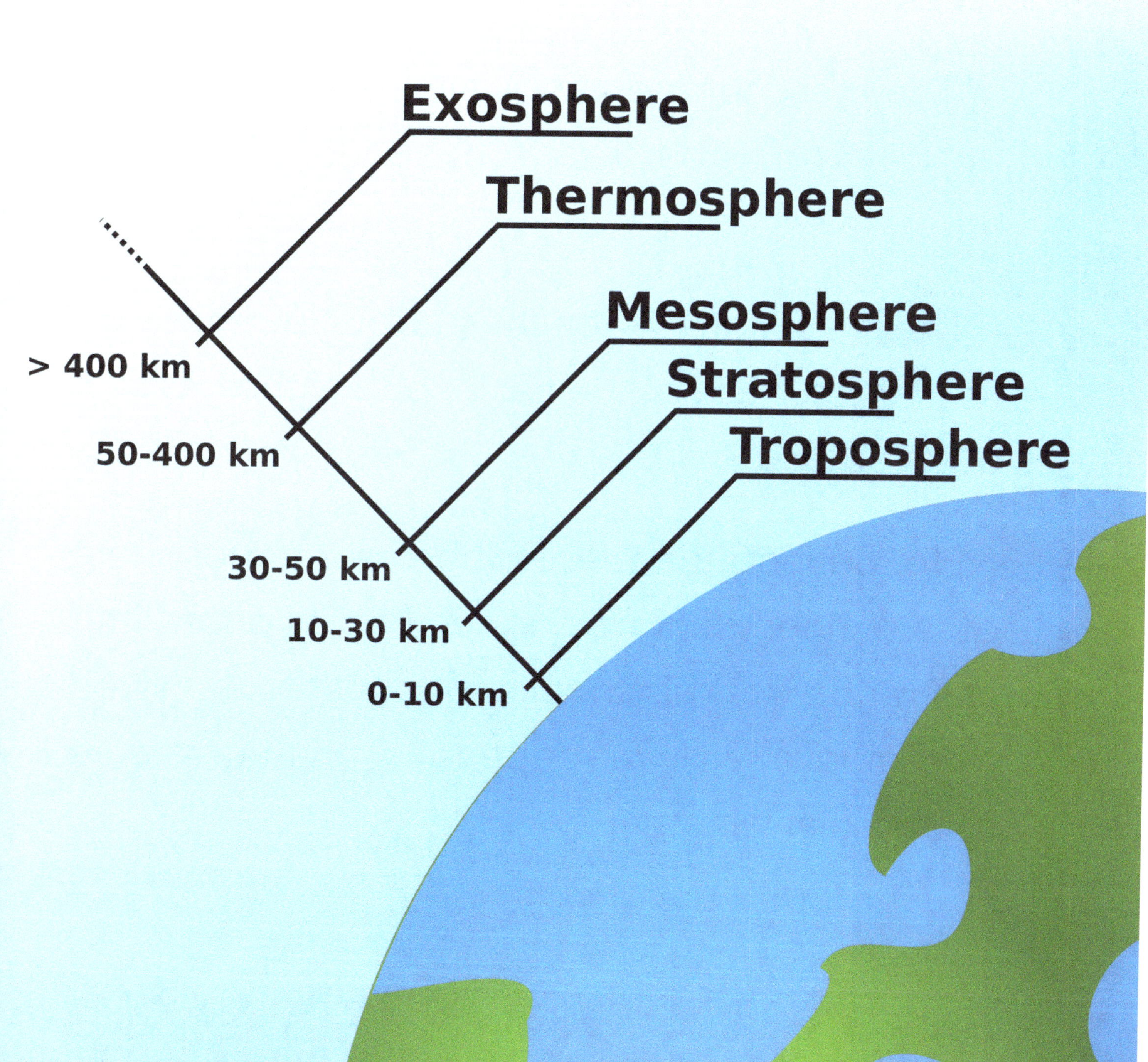

Exosphere
Thermosphere
Mesosphere
Stratosphere
Troposphere
> 400 km
50-400 km
30-50 km
10-30 km
0-10 km

The mesosphere keeps all life on Earth from being bombarded from space. This is our outer defence.

The mesosphere reaches about 60 miles up from the surface of the Earth. Is this, then, where outer space begins?

No. Beyond the mesosphere our atmosphere gets thinner, thinner, thinner. But its outer limit can range from six thousand to just six hundred miles above sea level, depending on the pressure of the solar wind.

So maybe there's a better way of figuring out where "outer space" starts than by counting oxygen atoms.

Astronaut in space.

THE ARMSTRONG LINE

Doctor Harry Armstrong demonstrated that if you get as high as about 12 miles above sea level (The Armstrong Line), the vapor pressure in the thin atmosphere will get so low that, at the temperature of a human body, your saliva, tears, and even the liquid lining your lungs would start to boil away. At this height you could not survive without a pressure suit or some sort of sealed and pressurized vehicle.

So maybe the edge of outer space, unless we have a space ship, is a lot closer than we normally think.

Astronaut in space.

ASTRONAUTS

Astronauts are "people who travel through space". The United States space agency, NASA, says that anyone who travels more than fifty miles above the Earth is an astronaut. Maybe that's the frontier!

Theodore von Kármán and JATO Team.

WRIGHT

THE KÁRMÁN LINE

In 1967 the United Nations passed the Outer Space Treaty. It bans any country from claiming territory in "outer space" for itself. The treaty sets the limit of "outer space" at what is called the Kármán line, about 62 miles above sea level. Theodore von Kármán demonstrated that if you were in an airplane that height and moving fast enough to support yourself in the extremely thin atmosphere, you would be moving faster than orbital speed and would be moving further away from the Earth.

So if you are the ruler of a country and want more territory, now you know where "outer space" starts and where you should try making claims.

THE WIND-SPEED LINE

University of Calgary scientists measured wind speed in 2009 and found that at about seventy-three miles above sea level is the mid-point in the change in wind speed. That is where we find that "high wind" changes to the very fast movement, over 600 miles an hour, of charged particles outside our atmosphere.

Whether this is the edge of outer space or not, it is sure the line beyond which you do not want to try to fly a kite!

Space shuttle launching.

Entry into earth atmosphere.

RE-ENTRY LIMIT

NASA uses seventy-five miles as the re-entry limit for the Space Shuttle and other space craft like the SpaceX rocket. At this point the outside of your spaceship is starting to heat up from friction with the atmosphere.

So, coming from space, you can be pretty confident you are almost to "inner space" at this point.

Astronaut finding a bright beautiful star in deep space
(elements of this image are furnished by NASA)

FIELDS OF FORCE

Another way to look at space is to think of what most influences the space we are talking about. While we are mostly still bound to Earth, everything beyond whatever limit we set is "outer space". When we start traveling regularly to the Moon and Mars, that space will be more like our local neighborhood compared to what lies even further out. So we will need terms like these:

GEOSPACE

Geospace is the area around our Earth, where our gravity has a strong effect both to hold our atmosphere in place and to create an electromagnetic field around our planet.

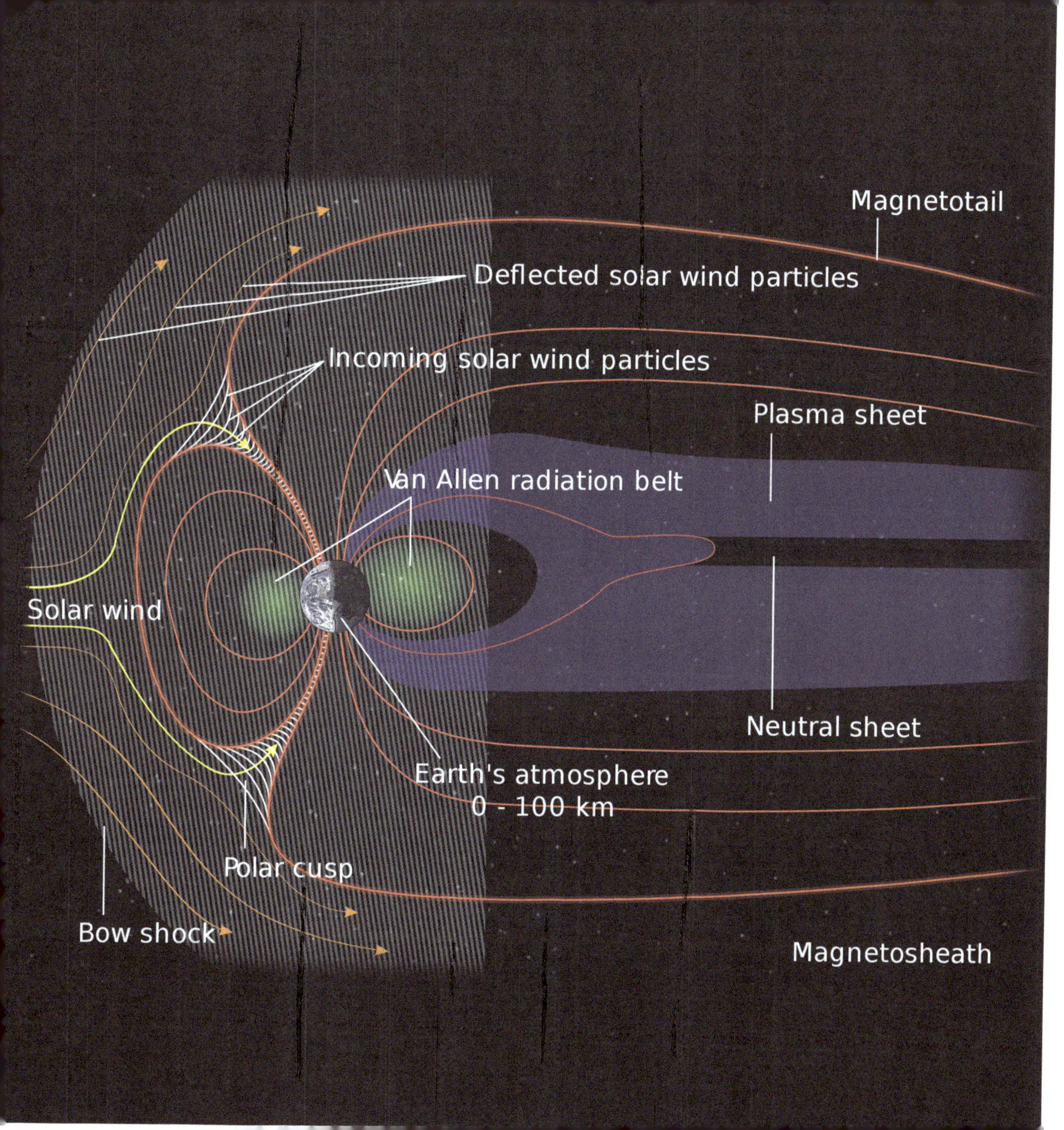

Magnetotail
Deflected solar wind particles
Incoming solar wind particles
Plasma sheet
Van Allen radiation belt
Solar wind
Neutral sheet
Earth's atmosphere
0 - 100 km
Polar cusp
Bow shock
Magnetosheath

CISLUNAR SPACE

This area extends from the center of the Earth to just beyond our Moon, and in this area Earth's gravity is still the dominant force.

Planet Earth and the moon.

INTERPLANETARY SPACE

Interplanetary space starts at the margin of our Sun and extends out to just beyond the orbit of Neptune, the planet furthest from the Sun. If the Moon and Mars make up our neighborhood, interplanetary space is our home town.

Earth and the planets around the sun at the center.

INTERSTELLAR SPACE

When we leave our Solar system and head toward another star system, we are in interstellar space. This area is huge, and mainly a vacuum, but there are charged particles, space dust, plasma, and even wandering planets that have escaped from their orbits around their home stars. We have not gotten into interstellar space yet, so we can barely guess what we will find there!

The cosmic cloud Orion Nebula - 1,500 light-years away from Earth.

INTERGALACTIC SPACE

Our Solar system is one tiny part of a galaxy called The Milky Way. Our galaxy is huge, and beyond it in every direction lie millions of other galaxies. The territory between galaxies is intergalactic space, and we have no accurate idea of what we might find out there.

THERE IS ALWAYS SOMETHING

Our Earth is a complex system floating through an even more complex universe. There is always more to discover here at home and in outer space! Read other Baby Professor books, *like Peeling the Earth Like an Onion* and *A Space Ride to Saturn!,* to learn more, both traveling in and traveling out!

Visit

BABY PROFESSOR
EDUCATION KIDS

www.BabyProfessorBooks.com

to download Free Baby Professor eBooks
and view our catalog of new and exciting
Children's Books